Travel Through Time

Flying High

Air Travel Past and Present

Jane Shuter

Raintree
Chicago, Illinois

Printed and bound in China by South China Printing Company.

08 07 06 05 04
10 9 8 7 6 5 4 3 2 1

Library of Congress Cataloging-in-Publication Data:

Shuter, Jane.
  Flying High : air travel past and present / Jane Shuter.
    p. cm. -- (Travel through time)
Includes bibliographical references and index.
Contents: Early flight -- Airships -- The Wright Brothers -- Earlyaviators -- Passenger planes -- Helicopters -- Going cheap -- Faster than sound -- Into space -- Staying in space -- Developing space.
  ISBN 1-4109-0579-9 (hc) 1-4109-0978-6 (pb)
  1. Aeronautics--History--Juvenile literature. 2. Air travel--History--Juvenile literature. 3. Space flight--History--Juvenile literature. [1. Aeronautics--History. 2. Air travel--History. 3. Space flight--History. 4. Transportation--History.]
I. Title.
  TL515S458 2004
  387.7--dc21

                2003010200

Acknowledgments
The publishers would like to thank the following for permission to reproduce photographs: pp. 4, 8, 10, 11, 16 Mary Evans Picture Library; p. 5 Taxi/Getty Images; pp. 6, 14, 18, 20 ATM Images; p. 7 Hulton Archive; pp. 9, 12 Popperfoto; p. 13 Royal Aeronautical Society; p. 15 Corbis; p. 17 Stone/Getty Images; p. 19 Hilary Fletcher; p. 21 ATN; pp. 22, 23 NOVOSTI; pp. 24, 26 Kennedy Space Center/NASA; p. 25 Johnson Space Center/NASA; p. 27 Jet Propulsion/NASA; p. 28 Langley Research/NASA; p. 29 Chris Butler/Science Photo Library.

Cover photograph of a 1920s airline poster reproduced with permission of Advertising Archive.

Every effort has been made to contact copyright holders of any material reproduced in this book. Any omissions will be rectified in subsequent printings if notice is given to the publishers.

Contents

Into the Air 4

Early Flight 6

Airships 8

The Wright Brothers 10

Early Aviators 12

Passenger Planes 14

Helicopters 16

Going Cheap 18

Faster Than Sound 20

Space Travel Begins 22

Staying in Space 24

Developing Space 26

Into the Future 28

Find Out for Yourself 30

Glossary 31

Index 32

Any words appearing in bold, **like this,** are explained in the Glossary.

Into the Air

People have always wanted to fly. The ancient Greeks told a story about a boy who made wings from feathers and wax. The boy, Icarus, flew too close to the sun. The wax melted, and he fell and died. Flying has always been seen as dangerous, too.

THE FIRST FLYING MACHINE?

Around 1485 Leonardo da Vinci, an Italian artist and inventor, began drawing flying machines. Almost 500 years later, in 2003, a machine made from Leonardo's designs flew a distance of about 325 feet (100 meters).

This is one of Leonardo da Vinci's drawings of a flying machine.

Just for birds?

It was a long time before people were able to fly. Birds use their specially shaped wings to fly. An airplane's wings work in a similar way. Airplanes called **gliders** fly using the movement of air. Gliders have no engine and have to go wherever the wind takes them.

People need a machine with an engine to be able to fly far distances. The engine gets the plane off the ground and keeps it going. The **pilot** can steer the plane. It does not have to follow the direction of the wind.

Today millions of people fly every year. They travel all over the world.

Early Flight

The Montgolfiers' balloon was made with painted cloth.

In September 1783, a hot-air balloon flew over Paris, France, for eight minutes. It was made by the Montgolfier brothers. The passengers, in a basket below the balloon, were a sheep, a chicken, and a duck. The next flight, in November, carried two people.

THE MONTGOLFIER BROTHERS

Joseph and Jacques Montgolfier lived near Lyons in France. They realized that hot air rises by watching how hot air from a fire carried scraps of paper up the chimney. They hoped that a lot of hot air caught in a balloon would lift people up.

In December 1783 another Frenchman, Professor Jacques Charles, flew in a balloon filled with **hydrogen gas.** Hydrogen is lighter than air, so it rises.

Dangerous flights

Early balloon flights were dangerous. The air in early balloons was heated by a stove in the basket underneath them. Their passengers spent much of their flight wiping the balloon with damp sponges because the paper and linen it was made from could burn easily. There was no way to steer balloons. They went wherever the wind took them.

This is a painting of the landing of the Montgolfier brothers' first balloon flight. The passengers included a sheep and a duck!

Airships

Balloons were difficult to steer and lift safely. In 1852, Henri Giffard made a steam-powered **airship.** It had a **rudder** on the back for accurate steering. The balloon made a 17-mile (28-kilometer) long journey at about 5 miles (8 kilometers) per hour.

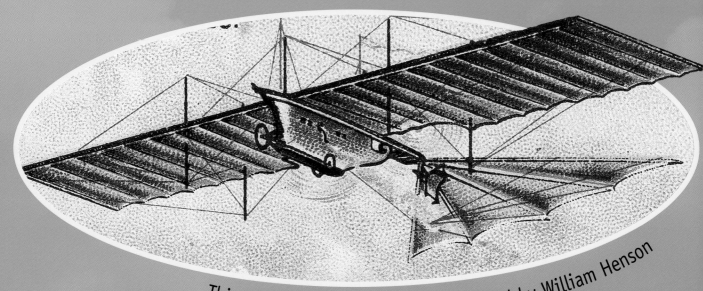

This aerial steam carriage was designed by William Henson in 1843. A steam engine provided the power.

Was steam the answer?

Steam engines needed heavy metal parts to stop the **steam pressure** from causing explosions. They were also very slow. Newly **invented** gasoline engines were lighter and quicker.

From 1900, **hydrogen**-filled balloons with gasoline engines were used mostly. The most successful were "rigid" airships. These had a wooden or metal frame covered with cloth, and were filled with hydrogen. Soon airships were large enough to carry carriages full of passengers underneath. They could travel a long way, even across the Atlantic Ocean.

THE *HINDENBERG*

The *Hindenberg* airship exploded in 1937, coming in to land in New Jersey. After this disaster people decided airships were too dangerous. Other inventors had been working on different ways of flying since about 1900.

This photograph was taken just as the *Hindenberg* hit a tower and crashed.

The Wright Brothers

Wilbur and Orville Wright made the first airplane to make a powered flight carrying a passenger. First, they worked on **gliders.** By 1902 they had a glider that the **pilot** could steer with cables. It flew for over one minute.

WILBUR AND ORVILLE WRIGHT

Wilbur and Orville Wright were born in Ohio in 1867 and 1871. Once they had **invented** the airplane they set up a business making airplanes and teaching people to fly. They traveled to Europe and around the United States giving flying shows.

This photograph of Wilbur (*left*) and Orville Wright was taken after they were famous.

On December 17, 1903, *Flyer I* took off, flown by Orville. It stayed in the air for 12 seconds. By the end of the day it was staying up for 59 seconds. Their 1904 airplane flew for about 5 minutes at speeds of 38 miles (62 kilometers) per hour. Their 1905 airplane stayed in the air for 38 minutes, 3 seconds.

Changing history

The Wrights' first flights were not big news at the time. **Airships** went farther, were faster, and stayed up longer. As the Wrights improved their airplanes, however, people saw that airplanes, not airships, were the best way to fly.

The Wrights' invention changed the way people travel forever.

Early Aviators

Between 1900 and 1945 flying turned from a dream into reality. At first airplanes were not very big and could only carry one or two people.

Charles Lindbergh is photographed here with the plane he flew across the Atlantic Ocean in 1927.

An uncomfortable flight

Early **aviators** (flyers) were very uncomfortable. The **cockpit**, where they sat, was small and cramped. They were not sealed off from the outside. The higher they went, the colder it got. They also had little space to store, or eat, food and drink on long journeys.

Flying was dangerous, too. Airplanes ran out of **fuel** and parts stopped working. Many things could make an airplane crash or, if the **pilot** was lucky, force it to land. Despite this, many aviators flew long, lonely journeys across oceans or deserts.

The first all-metal plane was the German *Junkers J1*, built in 1915.

AVIATOR FIRSTS

1909 Louis Blériot crosses the English Channel

1919 John Alcock and Arthur Whitten Brown make the first non-stop flight across the Atlantic Ocean

1924 First round-the-world flight takes five and a half months

1927 Charles Lindbergh crosses the Atlantic alone.

1932 Amelia Earhart makes the first solo crossing of the Atlantic by a woman

Passenger Planes

Airplanes were first used to carry mail. The first airmail service, in 1911, carried 6,500 letters from one part of India to another. Soon after this, airmail services zigzagged all over the world. Airplanes were useful for more than just airmail, though.

The Boeing 307, shown in this painting, was the first plane with air pressure control.

Farther, faster

From 1919, just sixteen years after Orville Wright's first flight, there was a daily passenger service between London and Paris. The first trip took 3 hours and 30 minutes. By 1933 passengers were using airplanes regularly, especially in the United States. The Boeing 247 flew 600 miles (965 kilometers) in 4 hours.

In 1938 scientists worked out how to control the **air pressure** inside an airplane. This allowed passengers to fly higher in sky. At the same time, scientists were finding ways of making air travel less expensive and more comfortable.

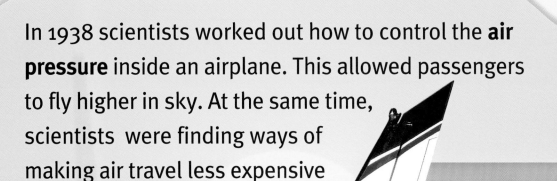

FLYING DOCTORS

Australia is a huge country. Many Australians live on farms that are miles away from any neighbor, let alone a doctor. The "flying doctors" were first set up in Australia in 1928. They flew to sick people in **isolated** places. The flying doctors treated 255 patients in that first year. Without flight many of these would have died.

Flying doctor planes are not very big. They only need room behind the pilot for a doctor, a nurse, and the patient.

Helicopters

Helicopters are machines that fly by using a **propeller** or **rotor** on the top of the machine. The rotor spins very fast. Early helicopters were hard to steer and keep balanced. However, they could take off and land without a long runway, so they could reach places that airplanes could not.

Early helicopters

The first person to **design** a flying machine that looked like a helicopter was Leonardo da Vinci, in about 1485. The first single-rotor helicopter was built by Igor Sikorsky in 1939.

The "autogyro" first flew in 1923. It did not go straight up, like a helicopter, and needed a runway.

Modern helicopters

Modern helicopters are much more stable. They can carry more people than early helicopters. They can also hover in one place. This means that helicopters are often used in sea rescues, where they can hold steady over the people being rescued.

NOISY ROTORS

Helicopters have serious disadvantages. They can be very noisy. The rotors and the engine together can make so much noise that people have to shout very loudly to make themselves heard.

Helicopters can be noisy, but they are a great way to see new places!

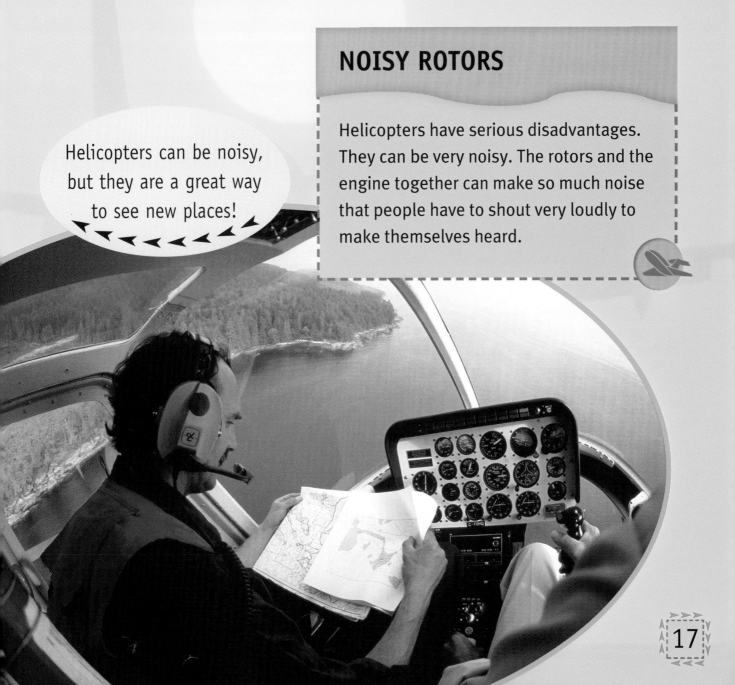

Going Cheap

After World War Two, more and more people made journeys by plane.

When World War II ended in 1945, a lot of **pilots** in different countries left the **air force.** Some of them set up small airplane companies all over the world. They used the airplanes, airfields, and equipment made for the war that were no longer needed. People could fly to more places than ever before.

JET ENGINES

Jet engines were **invented** in 1937 during the war, in both Great Britain and Germany. Airplanes used them straight away. Jet engines moved airplanes along much faster. After the war, improvements to the jet engine made bigger airplanes possible.

Since 1950, passenger airplanes have got bigger, faster, and cheaper. Bigger airplanes meant more passengers on each flight, which meant cheaper air fares. From 1960, more and more people flew on vacations to other countries. People flew for work, too.

Special planes

People used special airplanes in to reach difficult places. Seaplanes, for instance, were planes with boat-shaped feet instead of wheels. They were designed to land on rivers or lakes.

The Maldives is a country with many tiny islands. You can reach many of them only by seaplane.

Faster Than Sound

People wondered if jet engine airplanes could go faster than the speed of sound. This is the speed at which sound travels through the air. In 1968 Russian scientists flew the first **supersonic** passenger airplane. In 1969 Concorde became the first supersonic airplane in use. It was developed by the British and French. By 1976 it was flying a daily passenger service across the Atlantic.

Concorde had an unusual shape to cope with the speed at which it traveled.

SPEEDS

What is it?	How fast does it travel?
Sound	662 miles (1,065 kilometers) per hour
Wright Brothers *Flyer II* (1904)	38 miles (61 kilometers) per hour
Boeing 247 (1938)	190 miles (306 kilometers) per hour
Concorde (1970)	1,350 miles (2,172 kilometers) per hour
Boeing 747 (2000)	565 miles (909 kilometers) per hour

Supersonic problems

Supersonic airplanes were expensive to build and use. People objected to the noise and fuel pollution the airplanes caused by going faster than sound. Only sixteen supersonic airplanes were ever made. They are so much more expensive than ordinary airplanes that they have stopped being used.

Some companies stopped thinking about bigger, faster airplanes. Instead they made small jets for companies, or for people's personal use.

Space Travel Begins

In 1924 the first modern rocket was **launched** in the United States. It only reached 140 feet (43 meters) in 2.5 seconds before it ran out of **fuel.** Soon rockets were traveling for miles. Anything seemed possible.

Into space

People felt that it was only a matter of time before rockets reached space. During World War Two, governments gave scientists money to research rocket science. German rocket-powered V2 bombs caused a lot of damage in Britain during the war.

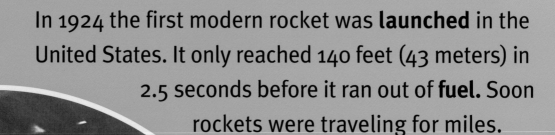

The Russian scientist Tsiolkovsky designed a rocket in the 1920s that he thought could reach space.

The Space Race

A "Space Race" began between the two most powerful countries in the world: Russia (then called the USSR) and the United States. Both sides were worried that the other side would get into space first. Scientists on both sides wanted to find out what space was like.

Laika the dog was the first living creature in space.

INTO SPACE

Some important dates in space exploration:

- October 4, 1957 Russian *Sputnik 1* goes into space, **orbits** Earth. Russian *Sputnik 2* is first flight with a living creature.
- April 12, 1961 Russian Yuri Gagarin in *Vostok 1* is the first man in space
- May 5, 1961 Alan Shepard is first American in space
- June 16, 1963 Russian Valentina Tereshkova in *Vostok 6* is the first woman in space

Staying in Space

In space, there is no **gravity** to hold things down. People float all over the place. This is called weightlessness. Space travelers, called astronauts, have to wear space suits that control everything going into and out of their body through tubes.

Moon landing

The moon is about 239,900 miles (384,400 kilometers) from Earth. In 1969 United States astronauts Neil Armstrong and "Buzz" Aldrin landed on the moon. It took four days to get there. The Russians had been the first in space, but the United States was first on the moon.

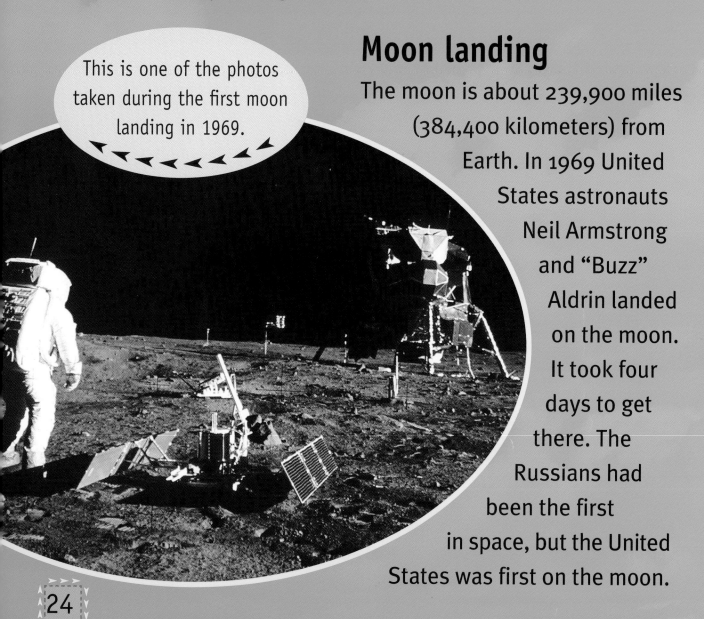

This is one of the photos taken during the first moon landing in 1969.

The next step in the Space Race was to find a way for astronauts to stay in space. Scientists thought that people would begin to live in space and on other planets. In 1971 the Russians **launched** a **space station,** *Salyut I*. It went around Earth on a fixed path called an **orbit.** Two years later, the United States launched their *Skylab* space station.

ALL TOGETHER

By the 1980s the fear of war between Russia and the United States was much less. The Russian space station *Mir*, launched in 1986, was mostly used by Russia, but astronauts from other countries were invited to use it, too.

This space shuttle is orbiting *Mir*, which looks smaller because it is much further away!

Developing Space

Once people had landed on the moon and stayed in space for long periods of time scientists began to work on other ideas.

Space shuttle

Early spacecraft could only be used once. A new vehicle, the space shuttle, was developed, which could be used for several journeys. In 1981 the United States **launched** the first space shuttle, *Columbia*. Several space shuttles were built and ran regular **missions.** Unfortunately, accidents killed space shuttle crews in 1986 and 2003. This led many people to ask if the shuttles should stop running.

The space shuttle looks like an airplane as it comes in to land safely.

While scientists are still excited about space, governments are less so. The Space Race had kept money pouring into space research. Everything about space research is expensive, like rockets, **fuel,** astronaut training. Governments put less and less money into it.

This photograph of space came from the probe *Voyager 2*.

UNMANNED PROBES

Governments have sent **probes** into space to explore far away planets. Probes are controlled from Earth and do not have people on board. This means they are cheaper and can go farther. The most successful ones are:

- 1962 U.S. *Mariner 2*, to Venus
- 1969 U.S. *Mariner 6*, to Mars
- 1977 U.S. *Voyager 2*, to Jupiter and Saturn
- 1989 U.S. *Galileo*, to Jupiter
- 2003 Four different groups are working on projects to Mars

Into the Future

Airplane flights are becoming more crowded every year. The airspace that planes fly in is filling up. People want to find a way to use space to make flying around the world quicker and safer. Using space would give planes far more airspace.

This photograph shows the HL20 space taxi. Scientists think that this is what small shuttles will be like, taking passengers from space airports.

SPACE AIRPORTS

Some scientists think that, far into the future, Earth might have several space airports in **orbit** around it. Large shuttles would go from one to the other. Small shuttles would take people to various airports on Earth.

Living in space?

It looks as if it will be a long time before people try to live in space. Neither space nor the planets have the water, warmth, or even the right kind of air. People living away from Earth would have to make their own "pretend" Earth. They would have to be sent everything from Earth for many years. Scientists still think that space travel and living in space would be too dangerous. This is what people once said about flying, so one day it could happen.

Some people think there may be water on the moon, but others disagree.

Find Out for Yourself

You find out more about the history of flying and space travel by talking to adults about how travel has changed during their lifetimes. Your local library will have books about the subject. You will find the answers to many of your questions in this book, but you can also use other books and the Internet.

Books to read

Maynard, Christopher. *I Wonder Why Planes Have Wings and Other Questions About Transportation.* London: Kingfisher, 2003.

Royston, Angela. *Extreme Survival: Space.* Chicago: Raintree, 2003.

Using the Internet

Explore the Internet to find out more about air travel. Websites can change, but if one of the links below no longer works, don't worry. Use a search engine, such as www.yahooligans.com or www.internet4kids.com, and type in keywords such as "airplane," "space shuttle," and "Wright brothers."

Websites

http://www.nasa.gov/audience/forkids/home/index.html
Visit the NASA website to find out more about space travel.
http://www.pbs.org/wgbh/nova/wright/
Find out about the Wright Brothers' first experiments.

Glossary

air force large group of soldiers who fight from the air, or support air fighters

air pressure way the air presses down on you the higher up you go

airship balloon with an engine, that can be steered and carry passengers

aviator person who flies an airplane

cockpit where a pilot sits to fly a plane

design plan or idea for something

fuel material used to power machines

glider plane with no engine that flies using the movement of air

gravity force that pulls everything towards it

hydrogen gas gas is something, like air, which cannot be seen. Hydrogen gas is very light and rises above air.

isolated far away from towns or cities

invent to make or discover something for the first time

launch force into the air

mission planned trip to space

orbit constant movement of one object around another

pilot person who flies a plane or helicopter

probe robot machine that explores space

propeller blade-shaped part of a ship or airplane that makes it move

rotor like a propeller, but fixed on top of a helicopter

rudder large oar at the back of a vehicle, which is moved from side to side to change direction and steer

space station place built in space that is made to have similar air to Earth. Astronauts can live there for a months or even years.

steam pressure way that water in gas form (like air) presses on a container if it is trapped

supersonic faster than the speed of sound, which is about 662 miles (1,065 kilometers) per hour

Index

air pressure 14

airmail service 15

airships 8–9, 11

airspace 28

Alcock, John 13

astronauts 23, 24, 25

aviators 12, 13

Bleriot, Louis 13

Concorde 20

dangers 7, 9, 13, 26

Leonardo da Vinci 4, 16

Earhart, Amelia 13

early flight 6–7

engines 5, 8, 9

flying doctors 15

gasoline engines 8, 9

gliders 5, 10

helicopters 16–17

Hindenberg airship 9

hot-air balloons 6–7, 8

hydrogen gas 7, 9

Icarus 4

jet engines 18, 20, 21

Lindbergh, Charles 12, 13

Montgolfier brothers 6

moon landings 24

noise and fuel pollution 21

passenger airplanes 14–15, 18, 19, 20

pilots 5, 10, 18

propellers 16

rockets 22

rotors 16, 17

round-the-world flights 13

sea rescues 17

seaplanes 19

space airports 28

space, living in 29

space probes 27

Space Race 23, 27

space shuttles 25, 26, 28

space stations 25

space taxis 28

space travel 22–29

speed 8, 20

steam engines 8

steering 7, 8, 16

supersonic airplanes 20–21

weightlessness 24

Whitten-Brown, Arthur 13

wings 5

Wright brothers 10–11